MW01273455

The Really, Really, Really Holy Night

Abingdon Press
Nashville

The Really, Really, Really Holy Night

ISBN 978-0-687-64577-0

07 08 09 10 11 12 13 14 15 16—10 9 8 7 6 5 4 3 2 1
Manufactured in the United States of America

Contents

The Promise of a Savior

Daughter: Papa, why are there so many soldiers in town?

Father: They are here to count us.

Son: Whatever for?

Father: The Roman government wants to know how many of us there are. They want to know how much tax to charge us.

Daughter: But Papa, we already pay taxes on everything! How can we pay any more? Why doesn't God do something?

Father: God will do something. God has promised to send a Savior, someone who will save us from the Romans and all the others.

Son: But when, Papa, when will the Savior come?

Father: *(sitting down in a chair)* A long time ago there was a prophet. His name was Isaiah.

Son: I remember him, Papa. They read from his scroll at the synagogue.

Father: Yes, they do. And he tells us that a time is coming when God will send a Messiah.

Daughter: But when, Papa, when?

Father: God doesn't tell us everything. Sometimes we just have to be patient. But when the time comes, this person will get rid of all the kings and princes who rule over us. We will be God's people, led by God and no one else.

Daughter: But doesn't Isaiah tell us when?

Father: Be patient, Daughter. It has been a long, long time since Isaiah wrote those words. We've been waiting for many years for a Messiah. The Savior will come in God's time.

Son: How will we know when the Savior gets here? How will we recognize this person?

Father: Isaiah tells us that the Savior will be a mighty one who will gather the people up like a shepherd carries a lamb in his arms. In this Savior, the glory of God will be revealed. We will understand God as we have never understood before.

Son: What a wonderful day, Papa. But why must we wait?

Daughter: It's so hard to wait!

Father: It is hard to wait. The children of God have been waiting a long time. But the Messiah will come. I promise because God has promised.

Based on Isaiah 40.

A Girl Called Mary

Mary: *(humming as she works)* So much to do today. I'd better get busy or I'll never be finished.

Gabriel: Greetings, Mary!

Mary: Who . . . who . . . who . . . are you?

Gabriel: I am an angel, and I have a message for you.

Mary: An angel? Why would an angel have a message for me? I'm nothing special.

Gabriel: Oh, but you are. God has found favor with you.

Mary: What do you mean, God has found favor with me? What have I done? What's going to happen to me?

Gabriel: Don't be afraid. God is pleased with you. You are going to have a son. He will be great. His name will be Jesus. God will make him king just as his ancestor David was king.

Mary: Wait! Not so fast! How can this happen? I'm not married yet!

Gabriel: The Holy Spirit will come down to you. Your child will be called the Son of God.

Mary: That's impossible!

Gabriel: Mary, Mary, Mary. Nothing is impossible with God.

Mary: Are you sure you've got the right girl? I'm nothing special. In fact, I'm rather ordinary.

Gabriel: Your cousin Elizabeth. . . .

Mary: What about my cousin Elizabeth?

Gabriel: Even though she and her husband are very old, they are going to have a baby, too. It will be a boy.

Mary: Elizabeth is going to have a baby—after all these years? How wonderful!

Gabriel: I told you, nothing is impossible with God.

Mary: What do I do now?

Gabriel: Nothing. It is already done.

Mary: I am the Lord's servant. Let it happen as you have said.

(Gabriel leaves.)

Based on Luke 1:26-38.

In Your Dreams, Joseph

A Story in Sound and Motion

Directions: Have one or more older children read the story lines together. Have another older child lead the younger children in each of the movements.

Props: jingle bells

Joseph was a carpenter in the village of Nazareth.
 (Make sawing sounds.)
Today he had worked very hard.
 (Make hammering motions.)
Joseph was very tired.
 (Droop and sag at the shoulders.)
He was glad when it was time to go to bed.
 (Yawn and stretch.)
Joseph fell asleep quickly.
 (Make snoring sounds.)
But it was a troubled sleep.
 (Make snoring sounds and restless movements.)
Joseph tossed and turned.
 (Put folded hands under left check and turn to left.)
Joseph turned and tossed.
 (Put folded hands under right cheek and turn to the right.)
Joseph was worried about what he had learned today. Mary was going to have a baby.
 (Sigh deeply.)
She said the baby was God's Son.
 (Pretend to rock a baby.)

Joseph didn't know what to do. That's why he couldn't sleep.

(Put folded hands under left check and turn to left. Put folded hands under right cheek and turn to the right.)

Joseph began to have a dream. In his dream he heard a voice.

(Ring jingle bells.)

It was the voice of an angel.

(Ring jingle bells again.)

"Joseph," the angel said, "listen to me."

(Shake finger as though scolding.)

"Am I dreaming? Or is this real?"

(Snore.)

"You are dreaming, but this is very real. So pay close attention."

(Ring bells.)

"You must marry Mary. Her baby is very special."

(Put hands on hips.)

"This baby will save his people from their sins."

(Stand up and shout, "Hooray!")

Then the angel went away.

(Ring bells.)

Joseph smiled and slept peacefully the rest of the night.

(Snore.)

The next morning Joseph knew the answer to his problem. He would marry Mary.

Together they would care for God's Son.

(Rock the baby.)

Based on Matthew 1:18-25.

An Emperor's Decree, a Baby's Birth

A Drama in Music, Scripture, and Overheard Conversations

Characters: Six Townspeople—male and female, mixed
Chief Priest
Pharisee
Scribe
Joseph
Apprentice
Mary
Innkeeper
Innkeeper's Wife

Props: baby doll wrapped in cloth

Scene: Center stage is a podium on which there is a large Bible. The Scripture Readers will come forward to this station and read the selections from the Bible (or a printed version of the Scripture). At the back of the stage is the Christmas Choir. The speakers will appear either stage right or stage left.

Christmas Choir:
Sing "O Come, O Come, Emmanuel" (Stanzas 1, 4)

Scripture Reader 1: A shoot shall come out from the stump of Jesse, and a branch shall grow out of his roots. The spirit of the LORD shall rest on him, the spirit of wisdom and understanding, the spirit of counsel and might, the spirit of knowledge and the fear of the LORD. (Isaiah 11:1–2)

(Three townspeople enter from stage right.)

Townsperson 1: Every sabbath in the synagogue they tell us God is sending a Messiah. But how long do we have to wait? After all, we've been waiting for a very long time.

Townsperson 2: Sometimes I feel that God has forgotten us. We pray for help, but none ever seems to come. First it was the Assyrians, then it was the Persians, then the Greeks, and now the Romans. How many more armies are going to march through our land?

Townsperson 3: God gave us this land. But we seem to be a doormat for every country on all sides of us. Surely if a Messiah were going to come, now would be a good time. Things couldn't get much worse.

Townspersons 1 and 2: Don't say that!

(All exit.)

Christmas Choir:
Sing "He Is Born" (Stanzas 1–3)

Scripture Reader 2: In those days a decree went out from Emperor Augustus that all the world should be registered. (Luke 2:1)

(Three townspeople enter from stage left.)

Townsperson 4: Registered? The decree is all about taxes, you know. The Romans don't care how many of us there are, as long as we are paying our taxes.

Townsperson 5: Taxes, taxes. That's all the Romans care about.

Townsperson 6: So true. They tax our food. They tax our children. They tax our land. They tax us when we come to the market. Pretty soon they're going to tax the air we breathe.

Townsperson 4: Don't give them any ideas. If they can find a way to do it, they will.

Townsperson 5: What do they do with all of our money, anyway? We don't see it being used here in Palestine!

Townsperson 6: They are building roads and aqueducts and maintaining armies.

Townsperson 4: Who cares about roads? We can't afford to go anywhere anyway.

Townsperson 5: Except to the towns of our ancestors to be registered.

Townsperson 6: Oh, yes, I forgot about that. This could be very inconvenient.

(All exit.)

Christmas Choir:
Sing "O Little Town of Bethlehem" (Stanza 1)

Scripture Reader 3: This was the first registration and was taken while Quirinius was governor of Syria. All went to their own towns to be registered. (Luke 2:2–3)

(Chief Priest, Pharisee, and Scribe enter from stage right.)

Chief Priest: We live in a time of peace.

Pharisee: But don't forget, it's a Roman peace.

Scribe: That's right. As long as we do what the Romans tell us to do, then we can live in peace.

Chief Priest: At least they let us worship at the Temple.

Pharisee: And we can make our own laws about our faith.

Scribe: But for goodness' sake, don't criticize the government. And don't cause any trouble, or you'll find yourself in prison!

(All exit.)

Christmas Choir:
Sing "O Come, All Ye Faithful" (Stanza 1)

Scripture Reader 4: Joseph also went from the town of Nazareth in Galilee to Judea, to the city of David called Bethlehem, because he was descended from the house and family of David. (Luke 2:4)

(Joseph and Apprentice enter from stage left.)

Joseph: Are you sure you'll be OK? I don't know how long I'll be gone.

Apprentice: I'll finish up the yoke for Jacob's oxen and then repair the door for the widow across town. Now, tell me again where you're going?

Joseph: I'm going to Bethlehem to be registered. It's a little town just south of Jerusalem. It's the birthplace of Kind David. King David was one of my ancestors.

Apprentice: How long will you be gone?

Joseph: It could be two weeks. It could be two years. Who knows.

Apprentice: What will you do for money while you're there?

Joseph: I suppose every town needs a good carpenter.

Apprentice: I'll keep watch over things while you're gone.

(Both exit.)

Christmas Choir:
Sing "It Came Upon the Midnight Clear" (Stanzas 1, 4)

Scripture Reader 5: He went to be registered with Mary, to whom he was engaged and who was expecting a child. (Luke 2:5)

(Mary and Joseph enter together from stage right.)

Mary: I know we have to go, Joseph. But tell me again how long it will take to get there.

Joseph: About three days, if we make good use of the daylight hours.

Mary: That's three very long, very hard days of walking. And that doesn't count the nights of sleeping beside the road. You do know that this baby is due at any time.

Joseph: I am aware of that. And I know you were looking forward to having your family all around when the time came for the baby's birth, Mary. But sometimes life gets in the way.

Mary: Not just that. I'm thinking of all the things we will have to pack to take with us! There's food for who knows how long. And water for the journey there. Not to mention things for the baby.

Joseph: Do you know the one I feel the most sorry for? The donkey!

(Both exit.)

Christmas Choir:
Sing "Once in Royal David's City" (Stanza 1)

Scripture Reader 6: While they were there, the time came for her to deliver her child. (Luke 2:6)

(Innkeeper and his wife enter from stage right.)

Innkeeper: Whew! I've never seen so many people in the town before. Every last room in the inn is filled.

Innkeeper's Wife: Not to mention the stables where the animals are kept.

Innkeeper: It's that decree from the Emperor—everyone must go to the town of the family's ancestors. Bethlehem is the city made famous by King David, the greatest king of all of Israel.

Innkeeper's Wife: There are many people from that family, that is certain.

Innkeeper: In fact, just a few moments ago I had to turn away a young couple. She looked as though she were going to have a baby at any minute.

Innkeeper's Wife: You didn't *really* send them away, did you?

Innkeeper: Calm down, I took them down below to the stable area where the travelers keep their animals.

Innkeeper's Wife: That place is hardly fit for the animals, much less people.

Innkeeper: I put down clean straw. They didn't seem to care. In fact, they seemed grateful that there was space of any kind at all.

Innkeeper's Wife: Honestly. What am I going to do with you! That poor girl. I think I'll carry some blankets and fresh food to them. At least one of us will show them some hospitality.

(Innkeeper and Innkeeper's Wife exit in different directions.)

Christmas Choir:
Sing "Away in a Manger" (Stanzas 1–2)

Scripture Reader 7: And she gave birth to her firstborn son and wrapped him in bands of cloth, and laid him in a manger, because there was no place for them in the inn. (Luke 2:7)

(Mary and Joseph take place center stage left. Mary is holding a baby wrapped in bands of cloth. Joseph is standing protectively beside her.)

Mary: Oh, Joseph, look how tiny he is. Look at his little fingers and toes.

Joseph: How can this be the Son of God?

Mary: He's got a lot of growing to do before he's ready to take that name. Right now, his name is Jesus. *(Mary kisses the baby's head.)*

Joseph: It's hard to believe that someone so small will someday do great things.

Mary: I just keep thinking about all that the angel said that day. Our son, our little baby, the Son of God, will someday sit on the throne of his ancestor David.

Joseph: He will reign over the house of Jacob forever.

Mary: And of his kingdom there will be no end.

Joseph: God is truly with us. We are blessed. The earth is blessed—or will be.

Mary: But right now, ssh. He's sleeping.

Christmas Choir:
Sing "Silent Night" (Stanzas 1, 3, 4)

Scripture Reader 8: And the Word became flesh and lived among us, and we have seen his glory, the glory as of a father's only son, full of grace and truth. (John 1:14)

Christmas Choir and Congregation:
Sing "Joy to the World" (Stanzas 1, 4)

(All cast members come to the center of the stage and sing.)

Shepherds Announce the Savior's Birth

Characters: Three Townspeople
Three Shepherds

Shepherd 1: *(to townsperson)* Did you hear the news? The Messiah has been born—right here in Bethlehem!

Townsperson 1: The Savior? Here in Bethlehem? How do you know?

Shepherd 2: The angels told us.

Townsperson 2: Angels? What would angels want with the likes of you?

Shepherd 3: We wondered that ourselves. We couldn't come up with an answer. But there we were . . .

Shepherd 1: Out on the hillside . . .

Shepherd 2: Keeping watch over our flocks . . .

Shepherd 3: And it was nighttime.

Shepherd 1: Suddenly they were there.

Shepherd 2: Hundreds and hundreds of angels.

Shepherd 3: The sky was filled with angels.

Shepherd 1: And they told us about the Messiah.

Townsperson 3: Did they tell you where to find the Messiah? I'm certain there were several babies born this very night.

Shepherd 2: They did. They said the Messiah would be wrapped in bands of cloth and lying in a manger.

Townsperson 1: Hmmm. That is unusual. Not many babies sleep in a feed trough.

Townsperson 2: That's for sure.

Townsperson 3: Is that all? Did you check it out for yourself?

Shepherd 3: We did. We had to see. And he was there . . .

Shepherd 1: Just as the angels had said . . .

Shepherd 2: In a manger in a stable . . .

Shepherd 3: And we saw his mother, Mary. We told her about the angels.

Shepherd 1: And now we're telling you.

Shepherds: The Messiah is born! Glory to God in the highest heaven and on earth peace among those whom he favors!

Based on Luke 2:8-20.

The Fresh-From-God Baby

Characters: Mary
Joseph
The Innkeeper's Boy
The Innkeeper
First Shepherd
Second Shepherd
Ruth, a traveler in the caravan from Nazareth
David, her husband

Extra Cast: Children's Choir

Props: box manger, baby doll, stuffed lamb

Scene: The Holy Family are at stage right: Jesus (a baby doll) in a manger, Mary seated behind the manger, Joseph standing beside Mary. The Innkeeper's Boy enters from left at a brisk walk, but stops stunned at the sight of the family in the spotlight.

Boy: *(astonished)* What's this? A baby? In our stable? *(turns to shout out left door)* Father! There's a baby in here! Did you know there was a baby here?

Innkeeper: *(enters)* I suspected there might be. You shouldn't yell around the baby, Son. You might frighten him. *(to the parents)* Or is it a "her"?

Mary: This is our son, Jesus. He is a very special baby.

Innkeeper: Yes, yes, of course. My wife says all babies are special. In fact, she is upset that I sent you out here. She asks if there is anything you need.

Joseph: You are very kind. We are warm and the baby is comfortable. We have no further needs.

Innkeeper: Well, I guess I had better tell that to the wife. She worries about a lot of things. Come along, Son.

Boy: Couldn't I stay here with the baby for a little while?

Innkeeper: As you wish. But don't bother these folks. They need to rest after their long trip and the baby and all. *(exits from left)*

Boy: *(goes forward to peer into manger)* I like brand-new babies. Some people say they are fresh from God. Do you think this baby is fresh from God?

Joseph: Absolutely! *(Sounds of voices approaching are heard.)*

Boy: I hear people outside. I had better tell those people to be quiet, since there is a fresh-from-God baby here.

(Two shepherds enter rather tentatively from left.)

First Shepherd: Is this where the baby is?

Boy: Shhhhhh. He has just been born. He is fresh from God.

Second Shepherd: We will be very, very quiet. We have come to worship him.

First Shepherd: *(to Joseph)* We were told by an angel to hasten to Bethlehem to worship a newborn babe. Is this the baby that is to be the Messiah?

Joseph: I, too, have seen an angel. This baby has been sent by God. He is to be called Jesus.

Boy: He is a fresh-from-God baby.

First Shepherd: Thanks be to God!

(The shepherds advance to the manger, where they kneel in reverence. Boy, slightly less reverent but visibly thrilled, peers over their shoulders for a moment, then picks up a little lamb—a real lamb would be wonderful!—and sits cross-legged near the manger.)

(The children's choir sings "Infant Holy, Infant Lowly.")

(Enter Innkeeper.)

Innkeeper: Is everything all right here? We saw strangers entering the stable.

Joseph: Yes, all is well. These brothers have come to worship the baby.

Innkeeper: It certainly is hard to keep track of things tonight. The town is filled with travelers, come to pay Caesar's tax. It's a hard time.

Shepherd One: *(rising to speak gently to the Innkeeper)* My friend, it is a blessed time. We have had a wonderful word from God!

Innkeeper: That so? You look like a shepherd, not a prophet.

Shepherd Two: Yes, we are shepherds. We were watching our flocks in the hills when we heard gorgeous music and an angel appeared to us.

Boy: I didn't see any angels around here. I guess they must have left after they saw the baby.

Shepherd Two: The angel was in the hills, Boy. The angel told us to come quickly to Bethlehem to see a newborn child, who is sent by God to be our Savior.

Boy: *(turns to Joseph)* You said an angel came to you, too. Did the angel tell you to come to Bethlehem to my father's barn?

Joseph: *(with a chuckle)* No, Boy. Caesar's tax men told us that. The angel told me that the child to be born to Mary is a holy baby, and that I would be responsible for helping Mary to take care of him. I was glad when the angel told me all this.

Boy: *(now turning to Mary)* Did you see an angel, too?

Mary: Yes, I did. The angel told me this holy baby was coming, and I said that I was willing to be the mother of this precious child.

Boy: A fresh-from-God child, and a Holy Child, too! Wow!

Innkeeper: Well, if everything is all right here, I'll get back to work. *(turning to Boy)* Now don't be a nuisance, Son. *(exits)*

(Enter Ruth and David, not speaking.)

First Shepherd: We must return to our sheep.

Second Shepherd: Sheep? God will take care of the sheep! I want to tell everyone what we have seen here! God has sent God's Holy One. I want everyone to know about it!

First Shepherd: Well, come on, then! The town is full of people! *(Shepherds exit.)*

Ruth: *(to Mary and Joseph)* We have been concerned about you ever since you left us to find a room at the inn.

Mary: Thank you. There was no room left at the inn, so the Innkeeper let us rest here in his barn. It has been fine.

Joseph: I had hoped to send word to the other families from Nazareth that all is well. Now I hope you will take word to our family and friends that God has blessed us richly.

Boy: This is a special baby, you know. He is a Holy One.

David: Probably a prophet. May we see him?

Mary: Yes, of course. *(Mary leans over and lifts the baby for all to see.)*

Boy: This is a fresh-from-God baby, and he is God's Son. The angels said so!

David: Certainly he is a fine baby. But I am not sure he is meant to be God's Son. Surely God would send God's Son to an important, rich family where he could be well taken care of.

Boy: These people are rich! They have a donkey, and Joseph himself was told by the angel to take care of this baby.

Joseph: Peace, Innkeeper's Boy. There are those to whom God will reveal this thing, all in God's own time. For now, let there be peace around the child and his mother.

Ruth: Yes, peace to this family. We just wanted to see the baby and to be sure that you are all right. Some on Bethlehem's streets have been talking to the shepherds by now, so you may have many visitors.

(Mary lays the baby back in the manger.)

David: *(peering into the manger)* Yes, he is indeed a fine young baby! You can be very proud of this baby. We won't bother you now. You must rest. We will let you know when everyone has paid the tax and we are ready to start back to Nazareth.

Joseph: Bethlehem seems like a nice village. Perhaps we will just stay here for a while so that Mary and the baby need not travel. I will be able to work as a carpenter.

David: Let us know, Friend. Good-night.

Ruth: *(to Mary)* May God bless you and your baby. *(Ruth and David exit left.)*

Boy: I have a great idea. I will stand at the door of the stable. When people come to see the baby, I will tell them that this is a Holy Child. I will tell them that you need to rest for a while. I will tell people that maybe tomorrow they will be able to see this fresh-from-God baby.

Mary: Thank you, Innkeeper's Son. You are a thoughtful boy.

Joseph: If we can find a small house in Bethlehem, we may stay for a while. We will be glad that you are near to help us, and to see the baby grow.

Boy: My father knows all about Bethlehem. He will know someone with a house. Now I will go and sit by the door.

(Boy gathers up his lamb again and exits left. Joseph may draw near to Mary, who rests her head on his side and sleeps. Children's choir sings "Silent Night," stanzas 1, 2, and 3.)

(See the play "The Best Caravan in the Whole World." These plays may be used separately for churches that have just a limited time period. For those wanting a longer play, "The Best Caravan" may become a second act for "The Fresh-From-God Baby." The Innkeeper's Son then becomes Simon, the neighbor boy. The role of the baby, of course, is changed to be played by a toddler.)

The Really, Really, Really Holy Night

(Please request no applause until the end of the pageant.)

Characters: Amos, an older shepherd with a beard: could be tween to adult

Micah, a young shepherd: a fifth or sixth grader

David, a young shepherd: also an older elementary child

Several small sheep: preschool, kindergarten, or first-grade children *(Cut sheep ears from construction paper and attach them to paper headbands for the children to wear.)*

Choir of elementary children *(seated on one side of the sanctuary near the stage)*

Simeon: older elementary child

Anna: older elementary child

Two wise men

A boy soloist

Several angels: first graders *(Have the same number of angels as you have sheep.)*

Scene: Amos and Micah sit around a small fire *(flashlight covered with red tissue paper, a few sticks)* at center stage. David, the third shepherd, stands near the sheep, his staff in hand. The sheep are clustered at right stage, with one or two of the sheep wandering around as though grazing. A quiet "Baaa" may be heard occasionally.

Amos: What a beautiful night. I love to be with the sheep out here.

Micah: Grandfather, when will we take the sheep to the fold?

Amos: When the weather is cooler, my son. Right now the sheep find it too hot in the daytime to graze. They graze better in the cool of the evening. See how Spot and Tipso eat while the lazy ones doze!

David: Still, the nights are long, Grandfather. Please tell us a story while the sheep graze. I will watch them while you speak.

Amos: What story? There are so many! Our people are the People of Stories!

Micah: Then tell the best one of all. You know, the night the angels sang.

(Elementary choir softly sings one verse of "Angels We Have Heard on High." Amos looks upward, as if remembering.)

Amos: *(nodding head)* Ah, yes. It was a night much like tonight, little wind, the stars ablaze above us, the sheep content after their hours of grazing. The other shepherds and I had just had a bit of bread. Old Caleb wrapped himself in his blanket, hoping to catch a wink of sleep while the sheep were quiet. *(falls silent)*

David: Come on, Grandfather! What next?

Amos: It's so hard to believe, yet it seems like yesterday. We were all dozing. Suddenly there was a brilliant light all around us.

Micah: Wow. Like a star falling?

Amos: Oh, no, brighter than that. It was as though the glory of God was shining all around us. We were frightened, let me tell you. Old Caleb kept his blanket over his face, and the rest of us flattened ourselves to the ground. We didn't know what to expect. But when we heard a voice, we looked up, and an angel stood before us.

David: That must have been a mighty busy angel, Grandfather. Are you sure it was an angel?

Amos: Oh, yes. The angel said not to be afraid, because down in the village a great thing had happened. The Messiah—the Lord!—had been born and was lying in a manger. And the music! You should have heard the music! I can hear it now.

(Now the elementary children's choir sings the chorus of "Angels We Have Heard on High" twice with usual gusto!)

David: I know the rest of the story. You left the sheep and hurried to Bethlehem, and there you saw the baby. Grandfather, did you know Mary and Joseph? Were they part of our tribe?

Amos: Yes, our people are descended from the great King David. Many of our relatives, whom we didn't even know, came to Bethlehem to pay their taxes. So while we shepherds didn't know Mary and Joseph personally, we knew why they had traveled to Bethlehem, and we remembered the promise that God would someday send a Savior to our people. Let me tell you, that was one awesome night!

(Children's Choir: "Silent Night," Stanzas 1 and 2)

(The Shepherds murmur to each other as they fall asleep gazing into the fire as the choir sings. When the song ends, the little sheep go to center stage to sing.)

Sheep: *(Sing to the tune of "Did You Ever See a Lassie?")*
Did you ever hear an angel,
An angel, an angel,
Did you ever hear an angel
Sing praises to God?

They sang of the baby,
The baby, the baby,
The baby in the manger
Was Jesus our Lord.

Did you hear the awesome singing,
The singing, the singing?
Yes, we heard the angels singing
Sweet praises to God!

They sang of the baby,
The baby, the baby,
The baby in the manger
Was Jesus our Lord.

(Gentle baaa's as the sheep return and cuddle down to sleep with the shepherds. As Shepherds and the sheep doze, Simeon enters from left, perhaps dressed better than the shepherds.)

Simeon: *(to the audience)* My name is Simeon, and I live in Jerusalem. I never heard the angels singing, but I can tell you something else about that baby they saw in the manger. Mary and Joseph brought Jesus to Jerusalem to be dedicated to God, as is our custom, when he was only eight days old. I had gone to worship at the Temple also, prompted by the Holy Spirit. *(pauses to look to left as Anna enters)* Oh, here comes Anna, one of our prophets. *(Anna approaches Simeon, walking slowly as though of great age.)*

Anna: What is it, Simeon? Are you telling that story again?

Simeon: Of course, I am! You can help me. There they were, Joseph and Mary and the blessed baby. God had promised me that I would not die until I had seen the Savior, and the Holy Spirit told me immediately that this was the child.

Anna: *(to the audience)* You should have seen Simeon! His face was radiant. Mary let Simeon hold the holy baby, and Simeon gave words of praise to God for sending the Messiah.

Simeon: Well, Anna, you praised God, too. And you told everyone you saw about the child who was sent for our redemption. We will never forget that day!

Anna: Hush, now, Simeon. I think these shepherds are waking up! Come along. *(Simeon and Anna go quietly out left.)*

(David stretches, looks at his sleeping companions, then rises and goes to the sheep. One or two look up at him while the other sheep continue to doze. David pets a lamb, returns to stand by the fire.)

David: That was the strangest dream I ever had. Sheep don't sing, do they? And I had forgotten all about Simeon and Anna. *(takes up his shepherd's crook)* I'll go see if any of the sheep strayed off while we slept. *(exits right)*

(Enter two Wise Men from the left as shepherds and sheep continue to doze.)

First Wise Man: Well, that wasn't all that happened! We astrologers knew about that baby king, too, although it was a few years later before we saw him. He was a toddler then. Mary and Joseph were so happy, living in that little house while Joseph worked as a carpenter to make a living. They certainly didn't realize that we were looking for their baby.

Second Wise Man: God sent that special star to guide us, or we would never have made it.

First Wise Man: Well, we almost didn't make it. That was a mistake, asking Herod for directions to the new king. Herod thought he might lose his throne, and that made him angry. He vowed to kill that baby if he could find him.

Second Wise Man: God was with us. The star led us to the Blessed Child and we worshiped him and gave him our gifts before going home another way. We didn't return to Herod!

First Wise Man: And Joseph took Mary and the baby and fled to Egypt. Herod never had a chance to destroy God's Son.

Second Wise Man: Now you folks know "the rest of the story," so we have to go. These shepherds are waking up. *(Wise Men exit left.)*

(Enter a boy soloist in Bible-times costume, singing "What Child Is This?" stanzas 1 and 3, perhaps accompanied by very simple instrument such as a guitar. After song, soloist exits.)

(Amos yawns hugely, then gently shakes Micah's shoulder.)

Amos: Time to wake up, my son. It is almost morning. I think David has gone to find water for the sheep.

Micah: But you didn't finish the Christmas story, Grandfather. We all fell asleep! Tell me, why do you think God sent the angels to tell the shepherds? We are not usually chosen to receive such good news!

Amos: Perhaps God wanted the whole world to know that Jesus is Lord of all, sent even to those of us who are humble. Someday everyone will know about this really, really, really holy night when the Messiah was born.

(Enter David.)

David: I have found water for the sheep. Only a few are grazing again. And the oddest thing happened—I think the sheep were singing!

(Children's choir again sings one verse of "Angels We Have Heard on High" as first graders, dressed as angels, come forward from the back of the sanctuary and take the sheep by the hand. Angels and sheep then stand at stage front to sing "Away in a Manger." At the end of the song, sheep and angels exit down the middle aisle, shepherds following. If desired, the Wise Men, Simeon, and Anna may come from backstage and exit with the angels, sheep, and shepherds, along with the children's choir. A pastor or leader steps to stage center to lead a prayer.)

Prayer: Blessed Lord, please accept our worship of song and remembrance. Come into our hearts, O Jesus, as we remember the day of your birth. Amen.

(Congregation stands to join in singing "Infant Holy, Infant Lowly.")

The Best Caravan in the Whole World
A Might-Have-Been Story

Characters: Joseph, a carpenter
Mary, his wife
Jesus, a toddler
Simon, a neighbor boy
A Wise Man with gold
A Wise Man with Frankincense
A Wise Man with Myrrh
Other Wise Men carrying chest or box
Camels and donkeys

Scene: At middle stage toward the back, Joseph, wearing a carpenter's apron, is busily planing a length of wood laid between two sawhorses. *(A plane is a hand tool once used to smooth wood by scraping off shavings. Many older carpenters or farmers still have them among their tools. Joseph probably used one. A "pretend" plane could be used if a real one is not available.)* Mary is at left front, seated on a low chair or stool, sewing on a piece of material. Jesus is playing at center front with some wooden toy animals or blocks. There is an extra chair and a low table at right front.

Simon: *(from offstage right)* Joseph! Mary! Come here, come here!

Joseph: *(amused)* It looks as though Simon has discovered something wonderful again. *(Simon bursts onto stage right.)*

Simon: Joseph, you should see what is coming! It must be the most wonderful caravan in the whole world! It is right at the edge of Bethlehem right now! I saw it myself!

Joseph: *(looking up from his work)* Hello, Simon! I'm sure you know all about good caravans. Tell me, what makes this one so special?

(Since the part of Jesus is played by a toddler, 2 or 3 years old, this child is free to do what comes naturally at this time: continue

playing or go to Simon, perhaps go to Joseph or Mary. If he goes to Mary, she may put aside her sewing to take him on her lap.)

Simon: *(still very excited about the caravan)* It must have been on the road from Jerusalem to Hebron. I can't imagine why it turned aside to stop at Bethlehem! We are so small compared to Jerusalem. What do you suppose they want, Joseph?

Joseph: *(laying aside his plane)* Simon, why is this caravan so exciting? You watch the caravans on the Jerusalem road all the time. Sometimes your father says you neglect your chores to run to the road. Isn't this just another caravan?

Simon: Oh, no, sir! This one has lots of camels, and lots of people wearing funny hats, and they have servants with donkeys carrying big boxes and bundles.

Mary: Simon, these are probably people from another country. They may have come to trade in Bethlehem.

Simon: I wish I could see what is in those boxes. Do you think they have money or jewels or maybe spices, or cloth, or . . .

Joseph: Who knows? But I would like to see this caravan!

Simon: *(goes to stage right to look out door)* Yes! Look, Joseph, look! They are coming down our street. Look at those camels!

Mary: *(rising, holding Jesus)* Perhaps Jesus would like to see the camels.

Joseph: *(moving toward the door to look out)* This is very strange. It is barely dark this evening, and already there is a very bright star shining. And yes! I do see the caravan. They are preparing to stop. *(turns to Simon)* Simon, we had better wait until morning to see these travelers. They are preparing to spend the night, and I think they must be very weary. Why don't you run along home now, and I will take you to visit them in the morning before they begin their trading.

Mary: Yes, in the morning we will take Jesus to see the camels, too.

Simon: Couldn't I stay for just a little while? I will be very quiet.

Mary: Of course. You may play with Jesus and his toys while I get bread and milk for our supper.

(Mary exits stage left. As the children play, Joseph hangs his plane from the wall or just sets it on the plank across the sawhorses. He removes his carpenter's apron and hangs it up also before settling into one of the chairs. Mary reenters carrying a pitcher and a loaf of bread, which she sets on the table. A loud knocking is heard at the door right.)

Simon: I hope that isn't my father. I want to play a while longer. *(Joseph rises, goes to the door.)*

Joseph: Come in, Sir. May I be of help to you? *(Several Wise Men enter. They wear turbans in the Eastern style and carry a large chest or box. See Matthew 2:11.)*

First Wise Man: We have come a long way, following a star that God put in the Heavens to guide us. It has led us to your house. We are searching for the one who is to be the King of the Jews.

Mary: We have no king here, only a small child sent by God. Come, Jesus.

(Jesus leaves toys and goes to Mary, who then seats herself and takes Jesus onto her lap. Simon goes to right door as the Wise Men move into the room. Simon looks out door to see the caravan, inattentive to what is now happening in the room.)

Second Wise Man: Please allow us to worship this Holy Child.

(Joseph goes behind Mary's chair, stands with one hand on her shoulder.)

(Wise Men kneel briefly before Mary and Jesus. Jesus may playfully reach out to touch a Wise Man's turban. Wise Men rise.)

Third Wise Man: Please allow us to give gifts to Jesus.

(Wise men who are carrying the chest or box set it on the floor and open the lid, and three of the Wise Men take gifts from the box. They approach Jesus and lay the gold, frankincense, and myrrh reverently at Jesus' feet. Simon has turned from the right door and watches this in astonishment.)

Joseph: Jesus' mother and I thank you for the gifts that you have given little Jesus. We will cherish them and we will see that they are used for Jesus.

First Wise Man: Thanks be to God, for we have seen the One of ancient prophecies. We have never seen a star like the one that led us here. Now we will return to our country, confident that the Chosen One has come to bless the whole world.

Mary: May peace attend your travels.

Joseph: Come, let me show you where to find water for your camels and donkeys.

(Wise Men bow again before Jesus, exit right with Joseph.)

Simon: Wow! Presents for Jesus! What is this one?

Mary: It is gold.

Simon: Gold is just given to kings. Is Jesus really a king?

Mary: I must ponder all this in my heart.

Simon: This one is frankincense. I have smelled it in the Temple in Jerusalem. Will the priests burn it in the Temple?

Mary: Perhaps.

Simon: This one is myrrh. I don't think those Wise Men brought anything to play with. I think Jesus would rather have had a ball or a toy camel or a sweet. *(to Jesus)* Don't worry, Jesus. I have a toy you can have. I will get it right away! *(bends to kiss Jesus on the cheek or top of head and hurries out right exit)*

(Joseph enters from right. Mary is still seated, holding Jesus if he is content. But being a toddler, it is okay if he wants to play or shake the gifts and so forth. Pianist plays "We Three Kings" very softly as Joseph kneels beside Mary's chair and takes her hand.)

Joseph: Now the whole world will know that this is God's Holy Child.

(Simon bursts into the room.)

Simon: Those three men aren't staying! Come on, come on! Come and see the camels!

(Joseph picks up Jesus and the three hastily exit right. After a moment, the caravan is seen by the audience. If a curtain can be drawn on the scene, the caravan can proceed across the stage on the outside of the curtain. But if there is no curtain, the caravan may simply come down the church aisle, across the front, and out by another aisle. Simon, Mary, Joseph, and Jesus stand to one side to watch the caravan. The piano continues softly playing "We Three Kings" until the parade is finished, whereupon the congregation is invited by the director or by Joseph to sing the hymn. As the congregation sings, the characters exit also, following the caravan of the Wise Men.)

(Caravan animals may stay in costume for a while to delight the children in the congregation. If a fellowship time follows the program, be sure there is a plate of animal crackers for the children to enjoy.)

Christmas With an Old Grouch

Characters: Henry, an Old Grouch
Kevin, his grandson
Emily, his granddaughter
Sam the Snowman
Richard, Santa Claus
George, pastor of the Old Grouch
Sarah, wife of the Old Grouch

Scene: Henry's living room. Kevin and Emily are playing a board game at a small table. Henry paces back and forth across the stage.

Henry: *(throwing papers into the air)* That does it! Bills, bills, bills. I don't know what this world is coming to: Christmas lights up at Halloween; shop, shop, shop all during Thanksgiving; buy, buy, buy on the television every single day. This is a bunch of baloney!

Kevin: Grandma said you were being an old grouch. You'd better quit that, Grandpa, or Santa will just skip your house.

Henry: *(glaring)* And you had better quit your nonsense.

(Emily gets up from the table and goes to Henry.)

Emily: Come on, Grandpa. Play Monopoly with us. It just might cheer you up.

Henry: MONOPOLY? That would just remind me of all the bills. And it would take a lot to cheer me up today. If your grandmother had my worries, she'd be an old grouch, too. *(looks out window)* Well, look at that. It's snowing. Now I suppose we will have to contend with slippery walks and blocked roads.

Kevin: *(to Emily)* Grandma is right. He sure is an old grouch today.

Emily: Look, Grandpa! Here comes some good cheer.

(Enter Sam the Snowman from the left. Sam has balloony pants and shirt, possibly stuffed with cloth or pillows, and some sort of snowman mask or carrot nose.)

Sam the Snowman: Merry Christmas, folks!

Henry: *(sarcastically)* Be careful. Don't melt all over the floor.

Sam: Oh, come off it, Henry. I just thought I would give you a laugh. What are neighbors for? *(pulls off mask or carrot nose; turns to children)* Henry's not laughing much right now. Is something wrong?

Kevin: Grandma says he's just being an old grouch. He's mad because of Halloween and Thanksgiving and bills.

Emily: I think you're neat, though. Why are you dressed like that?

Sam: Oh, there's a Christmas Walk around the Square tonight. I'm going to be making snowballs in one of the store windows— part of a winter scene, you know.

Kevin: Great! Maybe we can go to the Christmas Walk later. *(Henry scowls.)* With Grandma, I mean.

Sam: Well, I don't want to be late. Good-bye, kids. Good-bye, Henry. *(walks to door left, then turns to say to Henry--)* Time marches on, Henry. Better take time to enjoy Christmas. *(exits)*

Henry: The old busybody. I'll enjoy Christmas in my own way.

Emily: You don't seem to be having a lot of fun, Grandpa.

Kevin: Why don't we all go to the Christmas Walk? Grandma might want to go, too.

Henry: Do what you please. *(bends to pick up the papers he has scattered)* I'll just stay here. Christmas Walk! Bunch of nonsense.

(Santa Claus—actually Richard—enters from left.)

Santa Claus: Ho! Ho! Ho! Did I hear someone mention Christmas? Have you all been good this year?

Henry: Get lost, Richard.

Santa Claus: Ho! Ho! Ho! *(to the children)* Is Henry being funny?

Emily: No, he's being an old grouch. Grandma said so.

(Santa pulls off his beard and hat.)

Richard: Well, I'm not really Santa, but I hope to make some of the little kids happy, up on the Square. Better than being an old grouch, Henry. What's wrong with you, anyway? It's Christmas!

Kevin: Oh, he's mad about Christmas lights being on at Halloween, and people buying so much stuff at Thanksgiving.

Henry: Yes, I am! We have lost the real Christmas. All we have left is stress and bills, bills, bills.

Richard: Henry, we haven't even gotten to the real Christmas yet. Remember the Baby? Remember Christmas, when the angels sang, and the shepherds came to Jesus?

Henry: That's my point. Why all this other stuff, like a Christmas Walk around the Square?

Emily: That's extra, Grandpa. It shows we are happy about the Baby coming.

Henry: Well, I'll be happy when it's over.

Richard: He is an old grouch, isn't he? *(to Henry)* Come on with us to the Square, Henry. It will improve your whole outlook.

Emily and Kevin: *(retrieve coats from a chair, put them on as they say:)* Good-bye, Grandpa.

(They exit with Richard, who looks back at Henry and shakes his head. Henry paces the floor again, looking at the papers in his hand. The doorbell rings, Henry answers, and Pastor George enters.)

Henry: Pastor George, come in!

Pastor George: Hello, Henry. I hear you are an old grouch today.

Henry: You've been talking to my wife.

Pastor George: No, no. I saw your grandchildren just outside. But most wives think their husbands are old grouches at Christmas time. It comes with the season.

Henry: *(chuckles)* Well, you may be right. Cup of coffee, Pastor?

Pastor George: No, thanks, Henry. I just stopped to ask for some help with a Christmas mission.

Henry: Can't do it. Remember, I'm an old Christmas grouch.

Pastor George: I imagine Jesus knew some old grouches in his time, too. But Jesus never told the old grouches they could forget the needs of the world, did he?

Henry: I suppose not. You sure have a way with words, Pastor. What do you want?

Pastor George: I know you are good with a hammer, Henry, and right now I need a carpenter. We need help to do some repairs on a house. You remember the fire last week on 18th Street? That house is badly in need of some repairs before the family can move in again. I thought we could help.

Henry: Probably could help. Who's the family?

Pastor George: The Wrights. They have five children and have to stay in a motel until the house is fit to live in again. That's tough with five children, you know. Might need some cash for windows, too, Henry. Their insurance didn't cover everything. The folks at First Church are doing a great job, but our help is needed, too.

Henry: Wait a minute—FIRST CHURCH? That's not even our church. Hadn't we ought to catch up with our pledge to missions before we help folks from another church?

Pastor George: Henry, you just aren't thinking clearly.

Henry: You already know I'm a grouch.

Pastor George: That's the point, Henry. You aren't really a grouch at all. Think about it: Jesus had nowhere to lay his head, either. These children need their home, just as much as the baby Jesus did. So what are you going to do about it?

Henry: Okay, okay. What do you need? At least this feels Christmasy.

Pastor George: We need cash. We need help. We need someone to replace some broken windows and work on the kitchen, where the fire started. It's almost Christmas. I want those children to have Christmas at home, with games and love and security.

Henry: *(goes to table where children were playing)* Here, George, you can take this monopoly set to them. I'm sure our kids won't mind. *(hands the box to Pastor George)*

Pastor George: Henry, you are a case. Remember, the Wise Men brought precious gifts—gold, frankincense, and myrrh—to Jesus. Are you really only going to offer an old Monopoly game?

Henry: Yeah, and when they had given their gifts, the Wise Men departed for home, going another way to avoid trouble. I sure hope I won't be expected to give cash every time I turn around. You should see all the bills I have right now, George.

Pastor George: Yes, I have some just like them at home. Only right now this is about some bewildered children, feeling abandoned and frightened. It's Christmas. They have been uprooted, forced out of their home by the fire. You'd be jumping all over the place getting help if they were your grandchildren.

Henry: *(slowly)* You know, I think I might have an idea. Did you see a Snowman and a fake Santa Claus outside a while ago?

Pastor George: Yes, I did. They are headed for the Square, I'm sure. There's a Christmas Walk around the Square tonight.

Henry: That's the idea! Why don't we round up some treats and presents for those kids. Then I'll get Sam Snowman and Richard Santa Claus to take their show on the road. Maybe some of the others will come, too. We can all go work on the house, maybe have it ready in a few days.

Pastor George: Henry, you are a genius.

Henry: Sure, a grouchy one. But I think I have time to get a few treats before the Walk is over, and we can think of the other stuff later. We'd better hurry before the lumber yard closes. New windows first, I think.

Pastor George: It's going to cost money, Henry.

Henry: Yeah, yeah, I know. But it's beginning to feel a lot like Christmas. I don't mean to hurry you, Pastor, but we had better get started. *(pulls on coat and goes briefly to stage right to call)* Sarah! I'm going with Pastor George to see about some windows and some kids. Be back later! 'Bye.

(Henry and George exit. Sarah appears briefly on stage right.)

Sarah: Well! My dear old grouch found Christmas, after all!

Mr. Anderson's Christmas Project

Characters: Mr. Anderson
Mrs. Anderson
Jason, their son
Beth, their daughter
Shari, Beth's friend
Middle School Walk-Ons (many)

Scene: Mr. Anderson is seated at a small table, busy with pen and paper. Mrs. Anderson is seated in a chair reading.

Mr. Anderson: *(pumping an arm in triumph)* I've got it! I'm thinking of a Christmas project for the middle schoolers at church. They are such lively kids, you know.

Mrs. Anderson: That's why Pastor asked you to be their leader.

Mr. A: Well, I have a great idea. We'll all go up to Benny's to tour his hangar. He is repairing an airplane, and the kids can learn how to stitch a wing covering.

Mrs. A: *(looking up with disbelief)* A hangar? Stitch a wing? How in the world is that connected to Christmas?

Mr. A: *(somewhat deflated)* Well, you know. A hangar isn't so different from a stable, is it?

Mrs. A: *(shakes her head no)* You need to think some more. *(Jason enters from stage left.)* Oh, hi, Jason.

Jason: The guys are playing ball, and we got hungry. Anything to eat around here?

Mrs. A: You can have some of the Christmas cookies I baked.

Jason: *(calling out stage left)* C'mon, guys. Coast is clear.
(A line of middle schoolers enters, follows Jason in single file but with jostling and Hi's to the Andersons, and exits right, to kitchen.)

Mrs. A: *(sighs)* So much for the Christmas cookies.

(Middle schoolers file back from exit right to exit left, Jason last, eating cookies but carrying a bag. Jason holds up the bag.)

Jason: There is a homeless family under the bridge. We just thought we would take the rest of the cookies to them. Okay? *(exits left)*

Mr. A: Sure, sure, that's okay. Good idea.

Mrs. A: Beth said she would be home from college this morning, and she is likely to want cookies, too. *(exits right)*

Mr. A: I will have to keep thinking. That airplane hangar idea didn't seem to go over too well. *(bends over his paperwork)*

(Beth and Shari enter from left, arms full of packages.)

Beth: Anybody home for Christmas? *(Beth drops packages and hugs Dad. Shari stands still.)* Dad! Merry Christmas! Dad, this is Shari. *(Shari shakes hands with Mr. A. Mrs. A. enters from right.)*

Mrs. A: Beth! You're home already! *(hugs Beth, turns to Shari)* Hello, Shari. Do you live here in town, too?

Beth: No, Mom. Shari didn't have a ride home, so I brought her this far with me. It's another 50 miles to Shari's house. Her folks don't have a car, and there's no bus to Hiattsville. I need to take her home.

Mrs. A: I'll go with you. But let's have lunch first.

Shari: Oh, thank you! I didn't know what I would do!

Jason: *(enters)* Dad, you know the homeless family under the bridge? They are moving into a homeless shelter, but they can't get into the shelter until four o'clock. Could we take them some food and blankets? It's cold under the bridge.

Mr. A: The homeless family! That's what I was trying to think of! *(pumps an arm in triumph; turns toward right)* Dear? Is there enough lunch for a few more?

Mrs. A: Yes, I have plenty of stew. What is going on?

Mr. A: I will eat later on. Right now I am going to take food and blankets to the family under the bridge. Then I need to go to see the pastor about an idea I have. I have the perfect Christmas project for the middle schoolers.

Jason: I'm ahead of you, Dad. We could make that unused room at the church into a lounge where the homeless could be warm until the shelter opens, right?

Beth: I get it! With coffee for the parents, and games for the children, and maybe we could serve lunch. I'll help clean the room over Christmas vacation!

Mrs. A: *(fondly to husband)* I am proud of you, Dear. I know the congregation will love it. This is better than that hangar idea. You really are an angel. I will go pack up some food. *(exits right)*

Mr. A: Angel? Hey, that's an idea! We could go to Benny's hangar one afternoon. After all, angels and airplanes both have wings, right? That's a Christmas connection! *(Everyone groans.)*

Shari: Well, I think you are an angel, Mr. Anderson, and my parents will think so, too.

Jason: Yep, you're an angel all right, Dad. I am going with you to see the family and go to church.

(Mrs. A. enters from right carrying a small box holding bowls of food and gives the box to her husband. Mr. A. carries the food and blankets out stage left. Jason follows and waves his arms as though pretending to fly.)

Prayers

Eternal and loving God, Merry Christmas! We thank you for your Son, Jesus, the greatest Christmas gift of all, and we pray that our loving hearts make you happy, too. Please help us to share this gift. Amen.

Dear God, please bless all the people who have come here today to thank you and praise you. We pray that Christmas joy may be spread through the whole world and that all people will come to know your love. Thank you for Jesus. Amen.

Lord Jesus, come into our hearts today. Bless us as we tell the Christmas story once again. Gather us into the circle of your love on this holy day of your birth. Amen.

Almighty God, we know that you love us, because you have blessed us with your Son, Jesus. Help us to remember your holy gift all year long, and to act always as faithful disciples. Help us to think and act like Jesus, loving others and being kind to everyone. Thank you for Christmas. Amen.

O Quiet Night of Christmas

O Quiet night of Christmas,
That sweetly greets the birth
Of the Holy Baby Jesus
Who has come to bless the earth.

God sent him to a manger,
To humble people there;
That all the world might know him
And receive his loving care.

The Wise Men paid their homage,
The shepherds knelt with love;
The angels sang a birthday song
With choirs from above.

Today we greet the Baby
With songs of love and joy;
God sent the earth's Redeemer
In this Infant Savior boy.

Each child wants to serve him,
We each will do our part,
That all the world may worship him
With glad and open heart.

Speeches:
The Gifts of Christmas

(These short speeches are given by four children, each holding a large wrapped Christmas package, possibly with a large bow on top. On the bottom of the gift, however, is a large letter printed on pastel construction paper with a black marker which can be seen by the audience when the gift is turned over. These letters, one on each gift, are H, J, P, and L.)

First Child: One of the finest gifts of Christmas is HOPE. *(turns over gift so the H can be seen)* We cannot buy hope for any amount of money, but hope is given to us as a free Christmas gift by Jesus. Because Jesus came on this holy night, and because he was willing to lay down his life, we obtain the hope of a lifetime in heaven with Jesus. "May the God of hope fill you with all joy and peace in believing, so that you may abound in hope by the power of the Holy Spirit"—Romans 15:13.

Second Child: Another wonderful gift of Christmas is JOY. *(turns package over so that the J can be seen)* We feel joy because Jesus is with us. Jesus teaches us. When we read in the Bible about Jesus, we know that he loves us and is able to guide us through life and to give us eternal salvation. We feel joy in the love of our families, in our friends and neighbors, and in our church and Sunday school. Joy is in the air at Christmas time because God sent the greatest gift of all to the world, the gift of God's Son, Jesus. "The angel said to them, 'Do not be afraid; for see—I am bringing you good news of great joy for all the people: to you is born this day in the city of David a Savior, who is the Messiah, the Lord'"—Luke 2:10-11.

Third Child: Like all gifts, we must be willing to accept the gift of PEACE. *(turns package over so that the P can be seen)* Peace comes in many shapes and forms. Our whole being yearns for peace in the world, peace in government, peace in communities and in families. Jesus brings the Christmas gift of peace. This gift can lodge in each individual heart, and from our hearts peace will go out from Jesus to all the world. "Peace I leave with you; my peace I give to you. I do not give to you as the world gives. Do not let your hearts be troubled, and do not let them be afraid"— John 14:27.

Fourth Child: And the greatest of all gifts is LOVE. *(turns package so that the L can be seen)* God loves us so much that God sent Jesus, that we might have life forever. Jesus tells us to love one another, even as he has loved us. At Christmas time we especially remember God's love and thank God for the gifts of hope, joy, peace, and love. "And the greatest of these is love"— 1 Corinthians 13:13b.

All four children: We wish you the wonderful gifts of Christmas that Jesus brings to us: Hope, Joy, Peace, and Love. Merry Christmas!

(An additional ending may be used if there are many children in your Sunday school. Younger children may enter carrying the lowercase letters of ope, oy, eace, *and* ove *printed on separate pieces of light construction paper. These children can stand beside the H, J, P, and L packages to complete the words* Hope, Joy, Peace, *and* Love. *When the words are thus completed, all the children may then sing "Love, Love, Love.")*

ALL: It is Jesus' birthday! Merry Christmas!